Which Materials Float?

What's the Problem?

I0902125

Dale Dixon

COMPUTER SCIENCE For the REAL World™

Rosen Classroom™

Published in 2018 by The Rosen Publishing Group, Inc.
29 East 21st Street, New York, NY 10010

Book Design: Jennifer Ryder-Talbot
Editor: Caitie McAneney

Photo Credits: Cover Tatiana Bobkova/Shutterstock.com; p. 4 Villedieu Christophe/Shutterstock.com; p. 6 Perseo8888 /Shutterstock.com; p. 8 Nikki Zalewski/Shutterstock.com; p. 10 Cameron Whitman/Shutterstock.com; p. 12 Deniza 40x/Shutterstock.com; p. 14 Photo smile/Shutterstock.com.

ISBN: 9781538352021
6-pack ISBN: 9781508136712

Manufactured in the United States of America

CPSIA Compliance Information: Batch #WS18RC: For Further Information contact Rosen Publishing, New York, New York at 1-800-237-9932

Table of Contents

The Problem 5

Building Materials 7

Sinking 9

Floating 11

What Is Density? 13

Building Your Ship 14

Glossary 15

Index 16

The Problem

A boat is only as good as its **materials**. Some materials float on water, while other materials sink. Imagine you have to build a boat. First, you have to think about the problem you are trying to solve. How can you make your boat float?

Building Materials

Now that you know what you're trying to solve, you can get started. Look for different building materials. Materials include metal, wood, and rocks. The next step is testing each material to see if it floats or sinks.

Sinking

Pennies or paper clips are made out of metal. If you drop them in water, they will sink to the bottom. Rocks can be tiny pebbles or big stones. No matter their size, they will also sink in water.

Floating

Have you ever seen a stick floating by on a stream? Sticks are made of wood. Most kinds of wood will float. Boats have been made out of wood for thousands of years! Why does wood float on water?

What Is Density?

If an object floats on water, it is less **dense** than water. That means that its **matter** is not as tightly packed. If an object sinks, it is denser than water. Wood is not very dense because it has many tiny holes. It is **buoyant**.

Building Your Ship

You can solve your problem by using wood to build your ship. Now that you've chosen your material, you can make plans about the shape of the ship. It will be ready to float in no time!

Glossary

buoyant: Capable of floating.

dense: Tightly packed with matter.

material: Something from which something else can be made.

matter: Something that takes up space.

Index

B

boat, 5, 11

buoyant, 13

D

dense, 13

F

float, 5, 7, 11, 13, 14

M

material, 5, 7, 14

metal, 7, 9

P

problem, 5, 14

R

rock, 7, 9

S

sink, 5, 7, 9, 13

W

water, 5, 9, 11, 13

wood, 7, 11, 13, 14